Disc Golf

How to play and How to play better

Steve Pease

INTRODUCTION

When a ball dreams, it dreams it's a Frisbee.

1970s wham-o
bumper sticker

Thank you for downloading my book. I put this book together to help promote the game of disc golf. By spreading the knowledge of how to play the game better and have more fun doing it. Disc golf is a great game you can play at any age. The game is easy to learn, but takes a lot of practice to get good at it.

Have you ever wanted to give disc golf a try? Have you tried it but didn't know how to make the best shots? Do you play now and want to get better? This book is for you.

I have been playing since 1978, and I want everyone to enjoy the game and the sport as much as I have. My first-time playing was at Hansen Park in New Brighton Minnesota. They had the old cone style baskets, and I hated them, but the game drew me in for good. After that I played at Acorn Park in St Paul. This is still one of the most popular courses in Minnesota. Since then I have played most of the courses in Minnesota and many in surrounding states.

I have found over the 30-plus years I have been playing disc golf, there is no one good place to find all the information you need to play disc golf. You want to learn how to play, then learn how to get better when you master the techniques you are working on.

This book is my attempt to make it so new players can learn. And more advanced players can learn to improve. To have one place to get the information you need to play disc golf and then get better and improve your play as needed.

This book starts from the beginning and takes you through all the areas you will need to work on. It will give you all the information you will need to know to get better.

In the last chapter of the book, there are links to the best YouTube videos by top pro disc golfers. And the finest teachers on all the phases of disc golf, to help you get better.

Read the book and learn how to be the best disc golfer you can be.

Thanks for downloading my book. I would love it if **you left a review** about the book so we can get more people involved in disc golf.

If you have questions, you can reach me at mailto: steve@stevepease.net

or visit the site stevepease.net for more great books.

TABLE OF CONTENTS

Why you should play disc golf

"Learn to throw flat and straight, everything else works off of that." Ken "The Champ," Climo

Disc golf is one of the fastest growing new sports around the world. The sport of disc golf became a true game in the mid 1960s, when the game began being played at a few schools on the east coast. There is disagreement that the real inventor of the game was Ed Hedrick. He may not have invented the game, but he got the game started, and is known as the father of disc golf.

The quote above from the champ is so true. Learning the basics will get your game to the next level fast and with the least growing pains for you.

Disc golf has been around for 40 plus years and has been gaining popularity fast over the past 15 years. Many people are trying the game to see what all the excitement is about, and they are getting hooked on it. There are many reasons people are trying and enjoying disc golf, if you haven't played, you should.

I played when the sport was still in its infancy in the late 1970s. There were 5 courses in the Twin Cities, but there was only 1 good course. Acorn Park in Roseville MN, Acorn was the course I started to play, and I got hooked. Acorn park has changed over the years, but it remains one of the best courses in the Twin Cities, and still very busy. It is extremely busy on weekends.

So why should you try disc golf? Here are the top reasons you should try it if you haven't played, or if you haven't played for a long time.

- There is no age limits on playing disc golf. Disc golf is a lifelong sport. You can play when you're as young as 6 to 8 years old, and you don't have to quit until you can't walk anymore. There are a good number of players in their 70s and older that enjoy the sport. I plan on being one of them.

- Disc golf is one of the cheapest of any sports you can try. You can get the right equipment for a low cost, and play at a high level. The main equipment needed are the discs. You can get them for from $6 up to $20 each, with the majority of the top discs in the $12 to $15 range.

- There are also several good disc golf courses in the Twin Cities. At many of them, you can even rent discs to give the game a try. The Three Rivers Park District has 3 courses. Elm Creek, Hyland ski area, and Bryant Lake; you can rent a driver, mid-range and a putter for $2 per hour for all three discs.

- The cost of playing is also low. Most courses are in city parks and are free to play. The more challenging and better maintained courses are not free, but will only cost you $3 to $5 to play for the day.

- Disc golf is also great exercise and will help with your balance and coordination. Playing the average 18 hole disc golf course will cover around 2 miles. If you keep moving and throwing, you can burn a significant number of calories and even get a cardio workout. In a recent article at Healthstatus.com. They said a 200 pound person, would burn around

620 calories from playing 2 hours of walking and throwing.

- There is easy access to play disc golf in many areas, and there are more courses popping up every year. If you live in the Mpls. or St Paul area, you have access to over 100 courses within 50 miles from the center of the Twin cities.

- Not all areas have grown as fast as the Twin Cities. However there are many other areas around the country that the sport is growing fast. Many cities have good courses to play. The cost of construction is low so cities build them as a good investment and they are building more all the time.

- You can meet new friends playing disc golf. There are many people playing all the time. Many are looking for playing partners or others who enjoy disc golf. They are looking to share stories and memories with. Most players I've met on the course are friendly and having a good time disc golfing.

- There are more women playing the game, it's not for guys only. Women can be very competitive even with the guys. Strength helps, but finesse and technique are a very important part of the game. A great example is the Memorial tournament in 2014. Paige Pierce won the women's division with a score of -13. That score would have put her ahead of more than 80 guys in the men's division. That's impressive.

- Disc golf is simple to learn to play; the rules are

simple and you can learn them quick. The easiness of learning disc golf does not mean the game is easy to play. As with most sports, it takes lots of practice to get good. It takes many hours of playing to get to the point you will consider yourself good. You will never get bored because every shot is a different challenge.

If you've never played disc golf, or you played a long time ago, you owe it to yourself to try it. Disc golf is a lot of fun. It's challenging, good exercise, and you can play at almost any age. You can play it without spending much money. What could be better than that?

How to play disc golf

The 2016 World Disc Golf Tour is something we as touring professionals always wanted. A tour that focuses on being professional in all aspects. It's something that is needed if we want to progress as a professional sport.
Avery Jenkins

Disc golf is easy to learn, you may already know how to play. Disc golf is played much like ball golf, but you use a Frisbee style disc instead of clubs and a ball. Throwing a disc is something that most people can do with a little practice, unlike hitting a little ball with a club.

If you enjoy playing, you will get more serious about disc golf. You will find there are many choices of discs to buy that serve different purposes. There are other things you can get such as a bag made for carrying discs. A bag is not something you need to start out. As a comparison, you can buy 1 new big-name ball golf driver for around $400. That much money would buy your discs and a bag for many years. Or even for a lifetime.

How you play is simple. You throw a tee shot from the tee box on the hole. You go to where your disc landed and make your next throw with your foot behind the spot where the disc landed. There are small marker discs you can use to mark where your disc landed. Otherwise you can do what most non tournament players do. You can use the disc you threw on the previous throw. Just put your foot behind that disc as a marker.

Both ways are legal. If you want to get that extra 8 inches closer, you must mark it. Once you take the shot, don't forget to pick up your other disc or marker. You would think it's a no brainer. Although it happens to the best of us. You leave a disc lying on the ground and have to go back and get it.

You then repeat this process, throwing each time until your disc is in the basket.

In a group of players, the farthest from the basket throws first on the succeeding throws, the same as ball golf.

If your disc is in a bad place, or if it's behind something you can't get around. You can change your body position before you make the next shot. As long as one of your feet is in the position behind the marker disc.

You can throw the disc, overhand, underhand, sidearm, or backhand. You can roll it. You can throw it upside down. Straight up and over trees, etc. Anyway that works to get closer to the basket, but you can't step in front of the marker.

If your disc goes out of bounds, you have to take a penalty stroke, like in ball golf. Your disc is in bounds if any part of the disc is in bounds. You also have to take a stroke penalty if you lose the disc and you can't find it in a reasonable amount of time. If you find an out-of-bounds disc, or you lose a disc. You must bring it in bounds and play from the drop area, or the closest area to the out of bounds, but no closer to the basket.

If you land your disc in a tree, you can play it. As long as it's not higher than 6 feet from the ground. You can play the shot as if it landed on the ground below the disc. If the disc is higher than 6 feet, it is a penalty as if it went out of bounds.

You can get relief from some bad landings without a penalty, such as casual water. If there is water on the course, that is not a normal part of the course. You can take the disc out of the water and play it, as long as you don't go closer to the hole, like in ball golf.

There are rules that cover almost everything that could happen. You can read them on the official website of disc golf. **pdga.com/rules.** This will get you started and cover most issues.

Choosing the right discs

There may be people that have more talent than you, but there is no excuse for anyone to work harder than you do.
Derek Jeter

*When you first play disc golf, you face the dilemma of deciding which discs to use. There are over 300 discs on the market, which should you start with? Choosing the correct discs could determine if you continue playing and improving, or you will get frustrated and give up. If you buy the hottest and coolest discs on the market, you will get frustrated because you will not have the skill to throw them and make them fly how they should. **Do not buy the newest, fastest discs available when you're starting out.***

If you read any of the disc golf discussions in disc golf forums, one of the most talked about subjects from newer players is what disc do you use for _____? Fill in the blank for any shot you can come up. What is the right disc for a particular shot? The best disc for players in different stages of development is not the same. There is no one size fits all answer.

There are no right or wrong answers because everyone is different. Players are all at various stages of development. What works right for me, may not work for you. If you have a 200 ft. shot which has to go around some trees, you may use a mid-range. Better player would likely use a putter. Others players may use a fairway driver. It all depends on your level of control and what your abilities are. What you are comfortable throwing is also very important. If making a tough shot use what you can control best.

After playing for a while, you will find the right disc for most shots for you. In the example above, I would use a Discraft Buzzz. I can make the Buzzz do what I want it to do from 200 ft in. All my best approach shots have been with a Buzzz, many of them in the basket.

There are basics that are universal, but once you start playing, this is something you need to find on your own. Based on what you have learned and what works for you. We'll talk about some guidelines on where to start and how to decide when to move up to faster discs. Where do you go to get the best disc golf discs for you.

There are three main groups of discs, drivers, mid-range, and putters.

Drivers are the golf discs you use from the tee on most holes. They are the longest flying disc, and the hardest to learn to throw. When selecting your first driver, you should pick a disc that has a slow speed and is easy to throw. Not a distance driver, a fairway driver or a midrange is the way to start. Most of the newer drivers, are for more experienced players, and will frustrate you when you're starting out.

The recommendation for a first driver will differ from almost everyone you ask. My recommendation comes from many years of playing, and many years of throwing most of the discs that are available. A Discraft Buzzz, or Innova pro leopard, in a 160 gram weight, both are good starter drivers. They are not fast. However they are easy to throw and control, which is far more important than distance when you start out.

Midrange discs are for getting to the basket after the tee shot. My recommendation for your first driver is a midrange disc. When you are starting out, you will be able to throw it. It's a disc you will keep using as long as you play disc golf. The Discraft elite Z Buzzz or the Innova Roc. Once you have the lighter midrange figured out. Get a little heavier disc, or try a different model of a midrange that will give you more control in wind or other special situation.

The Buzzz or the Roc is the go to mid-ranges for most disc golfers. I'm not anti any disc manufacture. I use Discraft, Innova, Vibram and I even carry a Lightning disc in my everyday bag.

A putter is for shots from about 100 feet in. There are a lot of choices here that can be good. A putter is more of a preference. There are a hundred or more different putters to choose from. Made from many plastics with lots of different edge configurations. The recommendation for a good easy to use putter is to go to a store. Also check out the putters your friends use and see what feels good in your hand.

Pick a heavier weight, 170 to 175. Lower grades of plastic are better; they grip better in your hand and stick better in the basket. The higher-grade plastics are slippery and can miss because they don't grab the chains. I have used many putters over the years; you need to experiment to find the one that works for you.

As you play disc golf and get better, you will want to try newer faster discs. A Twin Cities local pro disc golfer and course designer **Timmy Gill** says. "Don't reach for the latest and greatest disc. Because your buddy throws a Surge 400 feet, doesn't mean you can. Start out throwing under stable discs, then move up to the faster wider rim discs." The driver is where most of the choices are. Resist the temptation to go to the fastest, newest drivers until you're ready.

The best way to know if you're ready for the next more over stable driver is when the one you are using turns over. Meaning it goes the opposite direction at the end of its flight then it did when you threw it at first. If you throw right handed backhand, the disc will turn left at the end of the flight. If it turns right, it is turning over.

When you go to a driver. My recommendations would be to try an Innova Monarch or Roadrunner. Or a Discraft Stalker or an Impact. I have a Roadrunner I use for a long turnovers or a hyzer flip disc because it flies a long ways.

When are you ready for the big fast drivers?

There is a lot of information to cover here in choosing discs. First, you need to understand the basic terms. A hyzer throw is when you release the disc with the outside edge lower. The inside is higher than the outer edge of the disc on the side that is touching your hand. Depending on how much hyzer angle is on the disc, it will go out, and turn toward the lower side of the disc.

The more the angle, the faster the disc will turn. In a flat release, the golf disc will hyzer at the end of the flight. If you are throwing a hyzer flip. Use an understable disc and release the disc on a hyzer. If you snap it, the disc will turn up to flat and give you a long s curve flight with added distance.

I have a #4 Lightning driver I can release close to straight up and down. With a hard snap that thing will flip up flat and go forever.

An Anhyzer is when the outside edge of the disc gets released at a higher angle than the edge in your hand. This flight will turn the opposite of a hyzer flight. If you want your disc to go the opposite way of what it would on a normal flight, release with a slight anhyzer.

The terms under stable and overstable get used often when talking disc golf discs. Under stable means that if you get enough spin on the disc, it will turn the opposite way of a normal throw (turn over). If you don't spin it hard, it will have a flat flight, and finish with a slight hyzer.

If you throw an Over stable disc without enough spin, it

will hyzer to the ground right away. A good player can throw these discs long and flat. A new player will throw it 100 feet and it will dive into the ground. If you are a new player try this. Find a friend that has a Discraft Nuke os or an Innova Ape and throw it. Then throw a Discraft Buzzz or an Innova Leopard. You will likely throw the Buzzz or the Leopard farther.

This is why you want to stay away from over stable discs until you can throw them with enough spin. You don't want your drives to go 100ft and then dive into the ground.

Getting the disc to spin fast enough for proper flight is called snap. When you learn to throw an understable disc with enough snap. You will be able to turn the disc the opposite direction of normal flight, and anhyzer. Called turning it over. Learning to throw an over stable disc with enough snap, will keep it from diving to the ground. it will also keep it in the air for a longer flight.

Once you throw with enough snap for the disc to perform the way it should, the under stable discs will turn over on you. Don't take them out of your bag. Being able to control a disc that turns the opposite direction of a normal throw, is a key part of a good disc golf game.

You're not ready yet to go to the fastest newest discs when you start. I know I keep bringing this up, because it is so important. You can shorten your time to getting better if you don't jump past the discs you should learn with. You are still working your way up to them. There are several flight guides to use to determine the next discs for you to try. **Discraft** has the simplest guide, but it gives the least amount of information. Negative numbers are under stable and the more positive numbers are more over stable.

The Twin Cities based **Gotta Go Gotta Throw** has a flight chart. It's called **Joes flight chart**, Joes flight chart focuses on how the disc will fly.

Innova has a good explanation of how their discs will perform. Don't get too hung up on one manufacture. Being the most successful at disc golf is finding the discs that work best for you.

The disc golf flight guide you should use when you are starting out. This guide is for if you don't understand what all the numbers mean. It is **the Marshal Street flight guide**. This is not the most accurate, but it is the easiest to follow. When you start out, you should use discs in the lower right part of the guide. When those discs turn over on you work your way up the right side and towards the middle. The hardest to throw are the upper left discs.

As you can see, the fastest newest discs are on the top left side of the guide. Stay away from there. When your beginner discs turn over, move up into the 5 speed discs in the C or D columns, such as an XL or XS.

These are all good tools to use to find a disc you need to for a particular task. Stay away from the over stable, fast discs until you have the snap to throw them.

Learning to play disc golf and getting to be your best is a process. It is a way of working your way up, start with the easiest and work to the hardest. A lot of those easier discs you will still use for some shots as you improve.

The five stages of a disc golfer

Persistence can change failure into extraordinary achievement." Marv Levy

Every disc golfer goes through stages from beginner to the top level you reach. After playing a few rounds, you get visions of a slow turning disc as it flies around the trees and lands under or in the basket. In reality, it takes many, many hours of practice to master the proper techniques. Making the disc do what you want it to do is not as easy as you think it should be.

One of the main reasons most of us don't pick up these skills as qick as they want is because they try to push ahead too fast. We don't learn the basic skills before we move to the next level. Patience is a big part of learning the proper techniques to become good at disc golf.

Human nature is not patient. Instant gratification is something we all want. You want to get where you want to be as a disc golfer right now. You will have a tendency to move ahead faster than you should if you don't have patience.

Stage 1 beginner. You start out thinking you'll give disc golf a try to see if you like the game. You play a few times and you either feel that the game is fun, or it's not your thing. If you like the game, you think all you have to do to get better is get the newest discs. Then you can throw longer drives, and get more control.

This is a mistake in the progress of your disc golf game.

You should focus on using easy to throw midrange discs. Learn to control the shots. Learn to shape the flight of the disc to perform the way you want it to. Learn to throw the easier discs straight and flat when you need to. You want learn how to get the disc within putting distance on approach shots. Generally approach shots are from 200 ft. in most of the time.

Once you master these shots, then go to the faster more over stable discs. Most things you do in life, you start out with easier to use, and beginner equipment. Learn the basic skills before going to more advanced equipment. It is critical in getting better, you need to learn basics first. Disc golf is no different. Everyone gets pulled into wanting to use the latest and greatest discs. Don't get sucked into this, and you will get better faster.

Stage 2 is the hooked beginner. If you don't like the game, you will give it up and never get to stage 2. If you advance to stage 2, which comes soon for most disc golfers. You feel you're ready for all the newest and fastest discs that the top pro's use. Fight the desire to skip steps, don't go to the newest and fastest discs that are being released. You're not ready yet, remember stage 1, learn the basics first.

Keep working with the midrange discs and get to the place you can make them do what you want them to do. If you watch the top pros, you see they will use a midrange Buzzz, or a Rock for shots that are up to 350 feet. Having control is critical. The more stable and slower midrange discs are much easier to control. When you can throw 300 ft. with a midrange or a fairway driver, then it's time to move up to the faster drivers.

In stage 3, you're figuring out what discs work best for you and how to control the discs you like. You have settled on your favorite type of plastic. You likely also have your prefered disc manufacture. This is a choice; all the top discs are similar in the way they perform. And the discs that work for you for certain types of shots. You learn that you like the feel of certain plastic more than others, and some models of discs work better for you than others.

Don't get caught up in the hype of only using one manufactures discs. I used Lightning and Innova discs when I started that was all there was then. I now like Discraft plastic better, I like the plastic better. I carry Discraft, Vibram, Lightning and Innova discs in my bag, every time I play.

In stage three, your confidence levels are up, you feel you are better than a lot of other players you see. This is where you tweak your shots and learn to throw longer drives. Now it's time to learn how to use the faster more over stable discs that will help your game go to the next level.

Stage 4 is where you are confident you are ready to play with the pro's. You may never play in tournaments, and you may never play against the top pros. However, if you get to this point and prefer to keep playing with your friends and go no farther, that is fine. I don't like the tournament play. It's too slow. I like to play fast and keep moving. When we play, we play two 27 hole rounds in about 4 to 4 1/2 hours.

Keep working on tweaking and improving your game and lowering your scores. Even though disc golf is a game against your opponents, it is also a game against yourself. I am always trying to beat my low score on every course. I also want to beat the guys I'm playing with. Continuing to improve, at whatever level you are at is the key to enjoying disc golf for a lifetime.

If you get to **stage 5, a pro disc golfer**. All the things you learned at the lower levels will stay with you to help you be successful. The opponents are better but the skills you learned at the beginning don't change.

Learn the basics at the beginning. Practice for consistency, and always strive to be better than you were yesterday. Disc golf is a great game and one you can play for a lifetime. Try to get better, play as much as you can, and always have fun when
playing.

Disc golf etiquette

Continuous effort — not strength or intelligence — is the key to unlocking our potential." Liane Cardes

Disc golf etiquette is important if we want disc golf to be seen as a serious sport to non-disc golfers. We need to remember when we play we are out there to have fun, and so are the other people that are playing disc golf and using the parks. Etiquette is just common sense and respect for others.

Some things may not offend you and the people you play with. They could be very offensive to other people. Many disc golf courses are in public parks. That means we need to use proper etiquette to make sure we can coexist with others in the park. Otherwise, they close down the course.

One important thing that all disc golfers should do is to read the **PDGA rules.** Follow the rules even when not playing in a tournament. The courtesy section deals with etiquette. Most of these are common sense. These are things we should all do to respect other disc golfers and other people using the parks.

Some basic etiquette rules to follow.

Let faster moving groups play through.
Don't talk while another player is throwing.
Don't move around if you are in view of someone putting.
Don't spit on tee pads.
Don't throw trash on the course, including cigarette butts.
Don't throw if you could hit someone in front of you.
Don't throw until non-disc golfers are clear of danger areas.

Don't yell obscenities, this is offensive to many people.
Vandalize nothing on the course or in the park.
Don't write on baskets.
Yell fore if someone could get hit by your throw.
Don't bring your dog to play disc golf, it is a distraction and slows play.
Don't play in groups bigger than Five players.
The player farthest from basket goes first.
If you find a disc with a phone number, call the person and return it.
Not everyone wants to hear your music.
Mark scorecard on next tee, not at basket to speed up play.

I have seen two courses closed in Minnesota in the past year and a half. Both shut down because of repeated vandalism, and repeated cases of not respecting others using the park and private property. Most disc golfers do not do these things, but we all suffer from the ones that do. Don't be the peson that hurt everyone.

If we follow the rules set forth by the PDGA. And use common sense in how we act when playing disc golf. We can coexist and grow the sport to be fun for everyone if we all practice good etiquette.

The Grip

What you lack in talent can be made up with desire, hustle, and giving 110 percent all the time." Don Zimmer

__Starting with the drive.__ The most used and best overall grip for driving from the tee on long shots is the power grip. The power grip is four fingers along the underside of the lip, and the thumb on top of the disc. Grip the disc tight for stability, and so you can control the exact release point.

There are several variations to the power grip most players use. If you learn the power grip, it is the best grip for most disc golfers to get the most control with distance. Here is a great website that goes over the top grips with pictures to help you get it right.

After you get the grip on the disc. It's very important that you get your wrist turned down when you're ready to throw and release the disc. If you don't get it turned down, you will release the disc way to high. It will go up, and stall, and you will lose lots of distance and control.

For midrange and control shots, I use a fan grip. The fan grip lets you have much better control of where the disc goes. And when you're not going for distance but control, the fan grip is much better and easier.

For putting I also use a slight variation of the fan grip. I spread my fingers farther apart to give more control. You're not going for distance so control is far more important.

Here is a link to a video that gives more tips on how to grip the disc to get the most out of it.

There are several other grips needed for specialty shots. We will get into more when we talk about the specialty shots in particular.

Approach and mid-range shots

The more difficult the victory, the greater the happiness in winning."Pele

Disc golf approach shots

Not everyone will agree with me on this, but if you want to lower your scores, the approach shots are the most important shots in disc golf. The best way to take strokes off of your game is to improve your putting and approach shots. As in ball golf, they don't get the focus that the drive does. Everyone loves to throw a drive 500 feet, and who doesn't want to sink a 50-foot putt?

If you can throw a drive 250 feet, then park your approach under the basket. All you will need is a drop in putt. It's a sure thing you will have better scores when you finish your round. This is true on wooded courses. My playing partners are all younger than me. Several of them drive longer than I can, but I beat them because my approach shots are much more accurate.

Many courses need finesse on many approach shots to get close to the basket. Learn to throw a mid-range disc around objects or flat and straight, and make it land close to the basket. Learn to make the disc turn right or left to get around obstacles. This will have a huge effect on lowering your scores. Most of the holes you will play in disc golf will be shorter than 500 feet. Landing the disc close on the second shot is the key to pars and birdies.

It would be awesome to throw a driver 500ft, but in

reality, the places where that will help your scores are rare. I'm not saying you shouldn't try to drive longer. I'm saying you should be able to get your second shot close before you spend lots of time working on longer drives.

2009 World Champion Avery Jenkins

2009 World Champion Avery Jenkins can throw a golf disc twice as far as most of us, he knows what he's talking about. Avery says, "One of the most defined skills of any pro player is the ability to throw accurate. And the skill to throw precise approach shots in any situation." Avery also said, "The ability to throw accurate approaches will benefit everyone's game. And will guarantee to lower your round scores."

The key to approach shots is adding them to your practice routine. It's much more fun to practice driving long than it is to practice approach shots. To lower your scores you will want to park the disc under the basket, or very close on any throw within 200 feet of the basket.

Putting is the second most important shot in the game. The skills you need to be better in disc golf are the same as in ball golf. If you perfect your game from 200 feet in, you will lower your disc golf score. And if you get a great approach shot on a long hole, you get a birdie.

Driving practice is important. Although you should spend the biggest part of your practice time on putting and approach shots. You will get more benefit out of your time spent, and you will improve your game faster, and lower your scores.

A good analogy of this is like the movie Tin Cup. A ball golf movie, where he played the round with only a seven iron, and still beat the guy he was playing. If you play the whole round with a mid-range and you drive only 200 feet. But you get your approach shots close, you will par most holes and birdie a few, and feel good about how you played.

How to putt better

I never left the field saying I could have done more to get ready, and that gives me peace of mind."   Peyton Manning

If you watch the disc golf pros, you see that putting is a big part of why they score so low. Slamming several puts over 30 feet in a round, can make a huge difference in

your final score. To improve your scores, putting is an essential part of the game to practice and improve.

There is no miracle putter, or any special way of putting that is better than others. The key is to find what works for you, and perfect your style and technique. There is no shortcut to getting better. The only way to improve is to practice and practice and then practice more.

The basic disc golf putt

The first thing is to find out what works for you. There are two main forms of putting, The straddle put, and the straight-line putt. Many players use one stance for close up putts and the other for longer putts. Some use the same stance for both long and short. Neither is right or wrong. They are both right in the right situation for different players. Straddle putting has never been something that has worked well for me; you could be the opposite. Find out what works by practicing both. Straddle putting is good to learn if you need to putt around objects in your way.

There are players who combine both types into one that works for them. The most important part is to make sure you have a solid stance, and you are not off balance when you are putting. A simple pre-shot routine you can go through each time you putt. This will help you to focus and not take nonchalant putts that cost you strokes. A pre-shot routine will also take away the tension and give you the confidence to make the putt.

Pre Shot routine

Your pre-shot routine should be a quick look at the shot.

Make sure you see obstacles in the flight path of your putt. Check to see whether the wind will have an effect. Visualize the disc golf shot going into the basket. Take a warm up shot or 2 without releasing the disc, to feel the release point. Pick a chain link to aim at. Take a deep breath and take the shot. This sounds like a lot to do. It should take less than 15 seconds to do this.

Release

When you release the putt, try to move your body as little as possible. Keeping your balance and stability is important in making sure the disc goes where you want it to go. Once you commit to the shot, don't analyze it anymore. Take the shot and be positive and confident.

Grip

The putting grip differs from the grip for driving. A fan grip or having your index finger outside on the rim of the disc is common.

There are several popular grips that good players use. This is something you need to experiment with to find what is comfortable and what works for you. The grip should be firm enough to control the release point, but relaxed enough not to overpower the disc. There is no right or wrong way to grip the disc as long as it works for you.

Practice

If you want to improve your game, you need to be in good shape, and you need to get your own disc golf basket. You can get a decent basket to practice with for around $100. After you get a practice basket, work on the things above until you find the best technique for you. Try several putters. Some people will try many putters before they find the right one.

Once you find the right putter for you, practice every day if you can. Practice will give you the confidence to not be tentative and put it in the basket. You will have the needed confidence; you will almost never miss a putt within 25 to 30 feet. It will make you a much better player. Mark Ellis from Discraft has a fantastic putting program you can learn and improve your putting. Check it out in the links at the end of the book.

Backhand Drives

You can motivate by fear, and you can motivate by reward.
But both those methods are only temporary. The only
lasting thing is self-motivation."
                              Homer Rice

Backhand drive. *There are few good players who are
not backhand dominant from the tee box. There are 6
parts to a backhand drive, they are grip, stance, reach
back, pull through, footwork and follow through.*

There is not much disagreement that the best grip for a
good backhand drive is a variation of the power grip.
There are several variations on the power grip that the top
pro's use, but they are still a power grip. Learn to use the
power grip on your drives. Watch the video by Dave
Feldberg at the end of the book and learn to use the power

grip for your backhand drives.

When talking about stance, I am referring to your disc golf stance at the point of release of the disc. For most shots you want to have your feet facing perpendicular to the target. And you want your front shoulder pointing at the spot you want the disc to fade at the end of the flight.

The reach back is one key to power on your drive. From this point forward a smooth and controlled throw is critical to a long controlled drive. You want to reach back as far as you can while staying balanced and in control of your body. Turn your head and shoulders as well to increase your reach back. Your weight should be on your rear foot at this point.

Getting from the reach back to the pull through. This takes practice. It's the hardest part of the backhand drive. It takes time and work to synchronize your movement while staying balanced.

You want to start the turn of your head, shoulders and hips. As you turn, your arm will pull forward. Keep the disc close to your chest as it comes forward. When the disc gets to your shoulder, you need to snap your wrist and speed up the disc. At the point of release you want your weight to be on the front leg.

The run up for a backhand drive should start with one step forward. Then 2 steps, then into the X step to add more distance and power.

The final part of the backhand drive is the follow through. It takes a smooth and natural extension of the movement you completed in the pull through.

Watch the video links and watch the video at the end by Minnesota local disc golfer Dan Beto. Dan has a great way to show how to work through the steps in pieces, don't change everything at one time. Remember that smooth and controlled will get you the most distance and the most accuracy.

Get more distance on your drives

I've missed more than 9,000 shots in my career. I've lost almost 300 games. 26 times, I've been trusted to take the game-winning shot and missed. I've failed over and over and over again in my life. And that is why I succeed."

Michael Jordan

One thing that most disc golfers want to do are increase the distance of their drives. Throwing for extra-long distance requires a shot you use nowhere else. There are

two techniques that will give you your maximum distance. The first is the hyzer flip, which if done right will give an S curve flight. The other is the flex shot, which is an anhyzer release that also makes the disc fly with an S curve.

Average golfer

The average disc golfer can drive 250 to 350 feet. Getting longer than that will need the correct footwork, grip. Also the correct pull through, follow through, and one of these two distance techniques. The S curve gives you extra distance because as the disc loses spin, it continues to go forward. Instead of the hard fade and drop you get with a normal throw. You can get a hundred feet or more of extra glide.

Flex Shot

To throw the flex shot, you use an over stable disc and release the disc at about shoulder height. You release the disc on an anhyzer angle. For a RHBH throw, you release the disc pointing toward the left; the disc will go right at first because of the anhyzer. Then the natural turn of the disc will take over and bring it back to the left. The disc will lose speed and spin. But it will glide forward instead of dropping hard to the left like with a normal throw.

Hyzer flip

To throw a hyzer flip. You use an under-stable golf disc. You release the disc aiming left, with a hyzer angle. Sometimes up to 90 degrees, depending on how under-stable the disc is. Most discs will need a release angle of 25 to 45 degrees; you need to determine this for each disc and the way you throw. For a RHBH, when you release the golf disc, it climbs and flattens. As it spins slower, the disc will turn over to the right. Because it is going against the normal fade of the disc, it will continue gliding forward, not fade hard. The disc will fade back with a normal end of flight fade. This will give you a much longer glide, it will finish going forward.

Conclusion

The pros don't all agree which way works best for the longest drives. Some like the hyzer flip, some like the flex shot. Most of the pros use the hyzer flip for their long drives. The correct footwork, grip, pull through, and follow through all are important. They each play a part in getting the longest drive you can get. Work on those parts of the drive before you try these techniques. Keep the wind in mind also; it can have a big effect on the throw. The best case is a crossing tailwind to help push the disc. There is a few videos to watch at the end of the book which will help you with those parts of the package.

Forehand drives

You're never a loser until you quit trying." Mike Ditka

The consensus of most of the stronger players is you need to have the pad of your fingers on the inside rim of the disc. 2009 Disc Golf world champion Avery Jenkins uses his version. He puts his middle finger pad on the rim and the index finger tip on the rim behind the middle finger. This holds the disc against your hand. Avery Jenkins technique is also my favorite. Other popular grips are with the pad of both finger on the rim, or the middle finger on top of index finger.

For most people, it works best to keep your elbow in close to your body. As you bring the disc forward snap your wrist as you release. As you release the disc, it is very important that you follow through with the palm of your hand facing the sky. The tendency when learning is to roll your wrist over. As you come through causing the disc to turn over and killing your flight.

Learn to throw the forehand standing still or with one step until you get the technique down. Once you're confident, you know how it works, you can add a run up.

The variations of how you can use the forehand are as many as the backhand. You are spinning the disc the opposite direction of a backhand throw. The forehand throws will go the opposite of a backhand. It will fill in most of the needed shots that are missing when you throw backhand only.

Learning to throw forehand will double the options you have in every situation to make the best shot. It will also help you get out of trouble without wasting a stroke.

Chapter 12 Finesse shots

Just keep going. Everybody gets better if they keep at it."
Ted Williams

Power shots in disc golf are important in play and practice, *but don't forget to practice your finesse and touch shots. There are 2 or three variations in power shots, but in finesse shots, there can be many variables you must take into account, so practicing these shots will lower your scores.*

In Minnesota and many other places around the country, we play lots of wooded courses. Trees challenge your ability to go over, around, under and sometimes through obstacles. Knowing what you can make the disc do is a valuable tool in your disc golf arsenal.

We have a tendency to ignore finesse shots when practicing. One reason is that they are difficult to practice. Set up obstacles to throw around and over and under. Work on the right shots in practice. There will be many opportunities to use the knowledge you learn to make tough shots. There are many places you need to take something off the shot to get it close.

The best way to practice finesse shots is on a course. Find a course that is not busy. Throw your discs into places that give you obstacles to make it difficult to get into the basket. Use several discs and try different techniques to get into the basket. Then when you get in a competitive round, you will know the shots you can make and what the best disc is to get you there.

You can also practice in your yard or a park if you have a portable basket. Find obstacles to get around and practice the same things as you would on a course. Even try your drivers on shorter shots. They will fade harder and may give you something that a midrange or putter won't. This will give you the most options to get you to the basket.

Know how to shape and bend your approach shots to the angles and distances you need. This will help your game and lower your scores.

How to practice

"Excellence is the gradual result of always striving to do better."   Pat Riley

Disc Golf Practice

As with most sports, disc golf brings out the competitiveness in the players. Getting hooked makes you want to improve so you can beat your friends. The best way to get better is to practice and play. How you spend your practice time will affect your scores. It will also show you how important practice is.

All practice is not equal. If you practice the wrong things, you will not get improve. If you want to get better at disc golf, try out my practice techniques, and you will get better.

Where to Practice

My favorite place to practice is on a soccer field. It is set up almost perfect for disc golf practice. The field is 360 feet long. It has lines at the 60-foot length from both end lines. It also has a circle in the middle. It is about 60 feet across. What this does for you is that it gives you accurate measurements. You have marked distances of 360 ft., 300 ft., 180 ft., and 120 feet. These are the perfect lengths to practice from. You can tell how far you are throwing and what disc to get you the distance you want.

If you have a portable basket, set your basket in the middle of the center circle and you have a 30 foot circle all the way around your basket for putting and practicing accuracy for approach shots.

Driving Practice

Everyone wants to drive the disc 450 feet or longer. That is a good goal to shoot for, but it will not help your score on most courses. Spend your driving practice time by practicing on the accuracy of your drives at the 300 foot length.

My recommendation is to spend 20% of your practice time on driving. Work on your grip and your release point the most. You should always use the power grip when driving. The key to accuracy in driving is releasing the disc at the correct time. Releasing the disc with the nose down, and getting the snap on the disc so you get it spinning fast enough. Watch the video at the end of the book to see the Dave Feldberg's hit training tip.

Stand at the goal line at one end; throw your drives at the goal on the other end of the field. Try to keep the disc flight side to side, inside the width of the nets. Throw it as far as you can throw it keeping it inside the soccer net width. Take 5 or six drivers and throw them. When you walk down to get them, you can tell how far your drives were and how accurate they were. Then pick them up and throw back from the other end.

If you want to go shorter, move up to the next line from the goal line, that line is 300 ft. from the other goal. Practice your hyzer and anhyzer shots by turning your body. Use the goal as your accuracy gage. Face at an angle away from the net and try to get the disc to land in the net. Go back and forth as long as you want. You will always have good feedback on distance and accuracy

Disc golf Approach shots

This is where you can improve your scores. If you have a portable basket, put it in the center of the circle in the middle of the soccer field. Stand in the net area and practice with your approach discs. It is 180 ft. from the back line to the center line. If you want to go shorter for practice, it is 120 ft. from the next line to the center line.

Spend 40% of your time practicing the approach shots. If you have a portable basket, you will also get your putting practice in at the same time. Learn to put your approach shots close to the basket. Work on ending up with 10 foot or shorter putts, you will have great scores. Test your discs, see which discs are best for different distance. Make them hyzer into the circle and anhyzer into the circle. You will improve your game fast.

Disc golf Putting

If you have a portable basket, you can practice on the soccer field. If not there are courses that have putting baskets set up. If you want to be a good putter, you should get your own basket. You should practice putting whenever you can. Even if you only have 15 or 20 minutes, practice putting. Practice from a variety of distances. Practice from different angles. Practice in the wind, from both sides with the wind blowing each way so you know what you need to do in those situations. Putting in a strong wind is the hardest shots you will encounter. Try to spend the other 40% of your practice time putting.

Conclusion

If you don't have a basket, the best way to practice is to find a field. Pace off 120 to 200 feet of space to practice approach shots to some item, you want to get close. Get to where you can throw the disc to the basket from 200 feet in, and you will drop a bunch of shots off your score. The best use of your time for disc golf practice is from 200 feet in. The approach shot is the key to getting better scores.

How to play when it's windy

Believe in yourself! Have faith in your abilities! Without a humble but reasonable confidence in your own powers you cannot be successful or happy.

Norman Vincent Peale

If you play disc golf, you know the most frustrating and most influencing weather issue you will face is strong wind. The wind can affect your disc golf game both physically and mentally, but there are things you can do that will lessen the effect, and allow you to use it to your advantage.

The first thing you need to do is assess the wind conditions before each hole. Look at the wind in relationship to the layout of the hole. The elevation of the area. Trees around the hole. These factors will vary the effect of the wind on your shots. Your assessment will vary every hole because of the factors mentioned above.

How do you approach driving in disc golf into a headwind. The best way is to use an over stable disc and throw it as a flex shot with lots of snap. Try to keep the release low by keeping your throwing shoulder low at release. Throwing approach shots into a headwind. Keep the disc on a nose down low flight path to maintain the most control. The more snap the better as this gives you more spin, lessening the winds affect.

Putting into a headwind is the toughest to overcome. Keep the disc low and nose down. If you get it up high, it will blow away from the basket. Don't be tentative, pick the spot and drive it into the basket.

A tailwind can work to your advantage. Use a more understable disc. Release the golf disc a little higher and let the air get under the disc and carry it. If you can throw a hyzer flip, this is the best place to use it. When throwing an approach with a strong tailwind, throw it low and with a lot of snap. Putting is also not affected much by a tailwind. If you keep the disc down and throw it into the basket with confidence.

A crosswind can also work to your advantage if you allow for the effect. If it is blowing the direction, your drive will turn, you need to allow the disc to turn farther than normal. If it is blowing the opposite direction of your normal turn, you can allow for less turn at the end. This is the same for drives, approach shots and putting.

If you think of the wind as something you have to deal with. Not something that will ruin your round. You can play in a strong wind and still play well. You must keep the **mental part of the game** strait, you can adjust to the wind and use it to your advantage. What you will see if you watch the top pros, they know how to use the wind and not let it beat them.

The wind affects putting more than any other shots. You can't be tentative when you putt in a strong wind. You have to pick your spot and drive the putter into the chains. If you try to ease it into the basket, the wind will make sure you miss.

The roller shot

There is only one corner of the universe you can be certain of improving, and that's your own self.   Aldous Huxley

When you see and hear players talk about throwing a roller shot, they are using it in a driving situation, and some people are good at it. It takes skill and a lot of practice to throw a roller and make it a useful driving tool. Using a roller on shorter shots is much easier to learn and make it effective. Not learning how to use a roller shot on midrange and approaches will cost you

strokes.

If you think about where to use a roller on shorter shots, you can come up with many possibilities. The most common place where this shot will help you is near the basket. Although many better players use rollers on drives. If you're in the trees or other obstacle you need to get around.

How many times have you got close to the basket and your disc goes into some woods close to the basket? To get to the basket the trees are blocking your flight paths. You try to sneak through an opening, hit a tree and you're still in the woods. The same situation can occur if you go off the fairway into the woods at any point. This is where a roller can help.

The key to making it work is to pick a spot outside of the woods where you can land the disc in the open and get it rolling. The disc will roll and turn in the direction toward the top of the disc. Hold the disc as you would a tomahawk or a thumber depending on which way you want it to turn. Aim for the spot and throw the disc so it lands on the edge. It needs to have enough speed to go the distance you need it to, and watch it roll to the basket.

In and around the Twin Cities there are many wooded courses where this technique is a part of how to get out of the woods. You can save strokes, on some of our tough courses such as Blue Ribbon Pines, Bryant Lake and Kaposia.

To do this, it takes a little practice to get the feel for how much the disc will turn. And how far it will roll, but it's easy to learn. Think about different places where you can use this shot. Learn to do it and it will save you strokes you didn't think you could save.

The roller shot will work for long shots and short shots. You should practice both to help you with problem areas. To throw a long roller shot you need an understable disc that will turn over for you. Grip the disc as you would a normal drive. When you release the disc you want to release it on about a 45-degree anhyzer shot. A forehand roller drive is the opposite. You want the disc to sail for a distance and come down on the edge and roll.

You need to allow for the disc to turn as it rolls. The disc will turn toward the top plate of the disc. If you throw right hand backhand. Land the disc to the left of the basket so it turns toward the basket as it loses speed on the roll. You need to practice this to see how the disc reacts. Learn how much your disc turns and how fast. Try different discs, all discs do not react the same.

If you're throwing a roller on an approach shot, you have a lot of options you can do. Read this article and watch the video for some good ideas. Learn how to use this shot for saving strokes on approach shots.

Other specialty shots

I'd rather attempt to do something great and fail than to attempt to do nothing and succeed.   Robert H. Schuller

In playing disc golf, there are two basic shots. The forehand and the backhand. Outside of the two main throws, are several specialty throws. Some are worth learning. Some specialty shots I would not learn unless you have perfected the rest.

Two other throws that are worth learning are the Roller shot, and the overhead shot. In many situations, they can be shots that can take strokes off your game. That is the goal of all disc golfers. These shots are at least worth checking out.

How to throw overhead shots

There are two types of overhead disc golf shots. The tomahawk and the thumber. Some player's use them for drives on normal holes; while most people use them for getting out of trouble spots. More accomplished players can throw these shots 500 feet or more. Howerver this is an exception and not the rule. Both shots are good shot to learn to take strokes off your game.

The difference between the thumber and the tomahawk is the flight path. The disc turn is the opposite of each other. The disc will turn over in flight so it will go upside down. It will then either go right or left depending on which throw you use, the thumber or the tomahawk. Later on, the throw will come back the other way at the end of the flight.

As an example. If you throw right handed and you are throwing a tomahawk. Hold the disc the way you hold for a forehand shot. You release the disc straight up and down. As the disc flies, it will turn to the right and be upside down. Then it will turn back to the left at the end of the flight as it's coming to the ground.

To throw the thumber, put your thumb on the inside rim of the disc, lay your index finger along the top edge of the disc. Both throws need a firm grip. The thumber will do the opposite of the tomahawk. If you are throwing left handed, everything above will be opposite.

Because the disc lands on its edge, it is risky to use these

shots if the landing spot is on the side of a hill. The disc
will have a tendency to roll down the hill. After the release
of the disc, you must follow thru. If you stop after release,
you will lose distance and will not get the desired effect.

These shots are difficult to throw. They take practice to
throw well. The reason you should learn them is that
sometimes you need to throw one to get out of trouble.
Even if you can only throw the disc 100 feet. It will still be
a useful shot to get out of trees or other obstacles that have
you trapped.

Once you learn the main disc golf shots. The backhand
drive, the forehand drive, and the anhyzer drive. Also the
hyzer drives and the approach shots. You should also learn
specialty shots that will get out of trouble.

Living and playing in Minnesota, and other northern
areas, where there are a lot of wooded courses. The
specialty shots will come to be useful. Most of the courses
you play in and around the Twin Cities have lots of trees.
You will find yourself in hard to throw from spots.

Playing wooded courses sometimes you get into tough
spots. Spots where you have no shot if you only throw with
standard shots. Roller and overhead shots can get you out
of bad situations. They can also save you shots if you can
control the flight of the disc on these throws.

The mental game

"I've never lost a game I just ran out of time."   Michael
Jordan

*A big part of being successful at disc golf is controlling
the mental game. Being able to control your mind and
focusing on the shot at hand is the key. Forgetting about
the past shots and not thinking ahead can make the
difference between an ok round and a great round.*

Your view of the round covers a wide focus on the entire
round and being able to look at it from a positive point of

view. Think about what you know you can do and not what you think will be problems. If you know you can only drive 300 feet. Drive 300 feet, then focus on being deadly from 200 feet in. Don't focus on not being able to drive longer. Focus on what you're good at and use that to your advantage. The mental game is every part of disc golf that is not physical. Course management is a big part of the mental game.

When you walk up to your disc or onto the tee box, decide where you want the shot to land. Then decide the best type of throw to get it to that spot, decide what disc will be the most likely to get you to that spot. Visualize the disc flight as it goes to the spot you want it to go to. Commit to making the shot and let it rip. Set up a routine like this to use on every shot.

Between shots engage in small talk with your playing partners. Think of a song, something to clear your mind of negative thoughts. If you made a bad shot, it's over, get it out of your mind and forget about it. You can't let one bad shot make you have another bad shot.

If you are throwing on a tight fairway, focus on what you know you can do. Step down to a fairway driver if you know you can throw that disc strait. Use the things you are good at. You will lower your score, and you will build your confidence, which will make you play better. Going for a shot you think you can't do will lead to higher scores and lower confidence.

Know when to play it safe and know when you have a chance to make the shot. Cale Leiviska, one of the top pro disc golfers from Minnesota says "Try not to compare your own game to top pros. You'll only feel down if you can't live up to that. This game is all about having fun and improving through repetition and experience. "

Use a pre-shot routine so you can get your mind in the right place for every shot. Forget about bad shots before you get to the next shot. Visualize the shot before you throw. Focus on the shot at hand, be positive in your mind, and play within your abilities. Practice shots outside of the round you want to do, so you can then feel confident enough to use them in the round. If you can do these things, you can win the mental game and make you a better player.

Playing disc golf in the winter

Many people say I'm the best women's soccer player in the world. I don't think so. And because of that, someday I just might be." Mia Hamm

When I say winter disc golf, I'm talking about winter in the northern half of the U.S., and other parts around the world where we have snow and cold. For many of you, winter is the nice time to play, when the nasty heat and humidity does not make it hard to breathe. If I could pick the best temperature for disc golf, I would have to say 50 to 70 degrees, no humidity, no wind, no bugs, and high sun, would be perfect.

Clothing for disc golf

The most important thing in winter is to keep warm, without being so restricted in movement, that you can't throw like you need to. I recommend wearing a polypropylene long underwear shirt. Wear a hooded sweatshirt over that, and a nylon shell as the outer layer, to stop the wind. I also wear a neck warmer when it's real cold, that I can pull up over my face. Wear a wool stocking cap. For my hands, there are a couple of things you can do. You can wear a wool mitten on your non-throwing hand. Or use a tube hand warmer like football players use, with or without a chemical hand warmer in it.

Or you can wear mittens on both hands, and take off the one on your throwing hand when throwing. I dislike to wear any gloves when throwing. I carry a pair of neoprene waterproof gloves in my bag, for reaching into cold water. I do the take off the mitten when I throw method.

For your feet. Make sure you have waterproof and warm boots. Don't wear too thick of socks. Your feet will stay warm because you are walking most of the time.

Other important tips

When there is snow on the ground that is more than 3 inches deep. I recommend using ribbons. I take some thin ribbon used for wrapping around gifts, use bright colors. Cut off pieces about 30 inches long. Some people say tape it to the underside of the disc. I prefer to tape it on the top, in the middle of the disc. Use a piece of duct tape. Make sure the discs are warm and dry when you tape the ribbons on, they will stay on much better.

Put your discs in the car the night before you play. This will get them to the colder temperature. That will make it so the snow will not stick to the discs if the temperature is close to freezing. If it's below 20 degrees, the snow will not stick.

Best winter disc golf Plastic

The best plastic for winter the best Discraft plastic is the FLX, or ESP. The Z and X plastics are OK.

The best Innova discs are the Pro plastic. The Champion seems to be very slippery when it is cold. The Star plastic is hard.

Why play in winter

If you play in winter, and you do the few things I have suggested. You will still have fun, and will keep in better playing shape for summer. Don't expect to score as low. There are benefits to winter play. There are no bugs, there are few tall grass areas, and the water hazards are much easier to deal with. There are only a few people on the courses.

How to play in the woods

"Disc Golf is more than a game"; "It can be a window that shows us how we interact with the world. The way we play is the way we live."
Patrick D. McCormick

The toughest types of disc golf holes are tight throws through trees. These holes require you to throw hard strait and low drives to get the disc down the fairway. However you need to be accurate enough to get through

the trees and keep it in the fairway. The best thing about wooded holes is if you are accurate and have touch, you can compete with younger stronger players and beat them. There are several things you need to be concerned with when playing in the woods.

Accuracy is more important than distance when playing in the woods. From the tee pad you should look at the hole and decide where you want to be when taking the second shot. Decide where you want the disc to land and focus on getting the disc to land on your spot. Don't only try to throw it as far as you can. Keeping your disc in the fairway is the key to shooting a low score. Especially if the woods off the fairway are thick.

Keeping the disc low is also very important. Throwing the disc high will almost always cause the disc to fade hard at the end of the flight. This will take it off the fairway and into the woods.

Learning all the different shots is important. When you go into the woods you will have to make shots from difficult locations. You will have them available to help you get out of trouble. Learning to throw overheads, rollers, forehands, backhands and other specialty shots. They will help you save strokes when you get in trouble. The more options you have available the better.

Know the limits of your abilities, sometimes you have to get it back in the fairway and go from there. Test tough shots and determine what will happen if you go for an impossible shot, will it be worse? Taking an extra stroke and getting back in the fairway may be the best option. It may be better than going for a shot that has a 10% chance of working. You can lose several more strokes if you hit a tree and go OB or farther into the woods.

If you play a wooded course, you will hit trees and lose distance on shots and get frustrated. When you hit a tree and get upset, get over it and figure out how to recover and get it into the basket. Being ticked off any longer than a few seconds will cost you more shots on the hole, so forget it.

The bottom line is to focus on accuracy instead of distance. Keep the disc low and when you get into trouble use all your shots to recover. Know when to get it back on the fairway, and get the bad shot out of your mind before you take the next shot.

How to avoid losing your discs

I always turn to the sports section first. The sports page records people's accomplishments; the front page has nothing but man's failures. Earl Warren

There are many ways to lose your disc golf discs. The most common ways to lose your disc golf discs is.

- To throw them into the woods or long grass and not be able to locate them.
- To play in winter and lose them under the snow.
- To throw them into water and they sink.

The throwing into the woods and long grass is the hardest to stop. If you do this, the best way to locate the disc is to see from landmarks that are stationary where it was last time you saw it. Try to pick at least 2 things you can visualize a relationship with. Then walk to that spot as straight as you can. There are options here, pay close attention to where the disc landed. If you do, you should be able to avoid losing your disc golf discs.

How to find the disc in the snow

My friends and I like to play year round. There are several courses in the area that leave the baskets in so we can play. Here is a trick I picked up a couple of years ago that works well, and will reduce the chances of losing discs.

Get some thin ribbon, used for putting around gifts. The 1/8 in. wide type. Pick the brightest colors you can find. Cut a piece of ribbon about 3 feet long for each of your discs. Take your discs into a room that is warm, and make sure they are clean and dry. Tear about a 2 inch piece of duct tape and tape the ribbon on to the top center of the disc. Push it down to make sure it is stuck on the disc good.

When you throw the disc it will go down into the snow, but the colored ribbon will be on top of the snow and you can find the disc. The key is to make sure the discs are warm and dry when you put the tape on. This tip has helped us avoid losing many disc golf discs.

Throwing into a water hazard

This one is also easy to avoid losing disc golf discs. You need to have a floating disc you can trust for shots over water. There are several floating discs on the market that work well. They vary for drivers, mid-range, and putters. I would recommend that you find one you can throw hard and have it do what you want. You also want to be able to throw it easier and have it do what you want. That way you can carry one floater in your bag. A good midrange or fairway driver that is slightly understable.

Here is a list of the floating disc golf discs on the

market for you to pick from.

There should be 1 of them you can use for most water shots.

Aerobie- Sharpshooter

Discraft- None that I could find

Dga- Blowfly

Ching - none

Gateway - none

Discwing - none

Snap - none

Millennium - none

Innova - Dragon dx, Hydra dx and rpro, 150g pro pig

Quest - Odyssey ultra, Odyssey power driver, Odyssey control. Odyssey midrange, crossfire, Raging inferno dt ultralite, Inferno ultra-light, Tbone ultra-light, Rockit ultra-light.

Lightning- #2 driver, #3 flyer under 170g, #1 slice under 170g. #3 hookshot under 170g, #2 hyzer, #3 hyzer, Rubber putter, #2 Rubber putter, #2 Roller under 182g.

The bottom line is to make sure you watch to see where your disc landed if it is in the woods or long grass. Don't count on your playing partners to watch it for you. Or always throw it in the fairway.

The winter trick works well. Once in awhile the tape will have to need changed, but I have had discs that the tape will stay on all winter. You would think it would affect the flight, but it has almost no effect on it.

Everyone should carry a floater, unless you play courses where water is not an issue. It also allows you to go for a shot you sometimes would not go for. It is worth the money. And most of the time when you go in the water, you go in close to the edge. Lightning discs are under $10 for most. So it is a very inexpensive addition to your bag. Don't lose your disc golf discs and you will have more money to buy the new ones.

How to work out to get better

We didn't lose the game; we just ran out of time. Vince Lombardi

Being in good shape will make you a better player. There are certain muscles that you will need developed more than others. Work on those and an overall workout to be your best. Stamina is also a big part of the game. If you're tired, you're not going to play well.

Disc golf workout

The goal of most disc golfers is to improve their game. To get better, you need to get lower scores. One way to improve your playing, and lower your scores, is to get into better shape. Getting stronger and more fit will help you in disc golf and many other areas in your life. The way to get stronger is to stress your muscles by making them work. I have developed a training program that will make you strong and fit. This will allow you to throw farther and to have fewer injuries. You don't need to have an injury from playing disc golf.

Workout for Legs

You may not think you use your legs for disc golf. Other than walking. Not true, your legs are an important part of your game. First, you do not want fatigue in your legs to take your focus off the shot and make you think about how tired you are. We all have been there; you are playing a game or a round, in any sport. It is hot, and you get distracted from making your best shot because you're tired.

The focus of the game is not what it was when you started. In your mind you want to get to the end. If your legs are strong and not fatigued you will continue to focus on the game. You will not focus on your body because you're tired. Strong legs are also important because much of the power in your shots comes from your legs.

Workout for the Core

The core is a big part of being stronger. The power from your legs must go through your core, to your shoulders and arm, to get to the disc. A strong core will also help you avoid back problems from the twisting motion. Like ball golf, your body goes through stress when you throw the disc.

Workout for Upper body

Your entire upper body plays a part in your strength and ability to get enough spin on the disc. The correct throwing technique is very important for distance. But strength also plays an important part. You need to have strong chest muscles, triceps, shoulders, and upper back muscles. Stronger and better developed muscles in these areas will help avoid injuries.

I used to have knee problems. My knees hurt me almost every day. One day I had an orthopedic specialist tell me. The best thing you can do to make your joints stronger is to strengthen the muscles around the joints. I worked on my Quads and built them until they were very strong. My knee problems went away. The knees have been great for 30 years. I also had a work related shoulder injury 6 years ago; the shoulder injury led me to work hard on my upper body. My shoulder got better, the pain went away. Even though the injured shoulder was on my throwing arm.

The Workout

This workout is not designed to make you big. It's made to make you strong and lean. That is what you need to help you play disc golf. It consists of 3 days of weight training per week. Each workout should not take you more than 45 minutes. You can do it with no equipment if you need to. I recommend that you get some dumbbells or exercise bands. If you need to lose weight, you should do cardio exercise on 3 other days of the week, take 1 day off. I recommend on your day off you play 2 rounds of disc golf.

Sunday Work chest, back, upper abs, and quads (upper legs). One exercise for each body part. Bench press, pull ups, crunches, and squats. Do bench press, then right to pull ups, rest for 1 minute. Second set, rest 1 minute, then set 3, etc. until you get to 10 sets. Then rest for a 2 minutes and do the quads, upper abs. Do the squats then right to the crunches, rest 1 minute, then set 2, etc. until 10 sets.

Monday Do cardio, to help build your stamina.

Tuesday, Triceps and biceps. Set 2 is shoulders and calves. Do like the Sunday workout. 8 reps of curls, 8 reps of triceps kickbacks, this is 1 set. Do 10 sets. Then do overhead press, and calf raises for 10 sets.

Wednesday Cardio

Thursday Thursday's you should work on the muscles you need the most work on. I do chest and back again. But change the exercise to push ups and bent over rowing. Then I do upright rowing for shoulders, and reverse crunch for the lower abs.

Friday Cardio

Saturday Play disc golf, 1 or 2 rounds.

Sunday Start over.

Disc golf workout

This workout will show noticeable results in a few weeks, and it doesn't take much of your time. Another huge benefit of working out for disc golf. If you are a hardcore player like me, who plays through the winter and snow. You need to be stronger in the winter. Most of your throws are from a standing position, no run up, because of the bad footing. Your throws will be much better if you are stronger.

Conclusion There is no downside to doing this disc golf workout. Being stronger and in better shape will help you in disc golf. It will help you in your everyday life, and will make you feel better.

To stay up to date on all disc golf news, check out Disc golf news blog.

Where to buy disc golf equipment

One day of practice is like one day of clean living. It doesn't do you any good. Abe Lemmons

There are hundreds of places to get disc golf equipment. You can get discs in a pinch at Walmart, Dicks Sporting Goods, and even at some gas stations near disc golf courses.

The best place to get equipment is online, unless you live near one of the top online retailers.

The top online retailers

Disc golf center is the top online retailer. The main reasons are you can get a discount that goes up the more you spend. You can select the exact weight and color of the discs you are ordering. They are also the lowest price or close to it.

Gotta Go Gotta Throw This is where I get most of my discs. The prices are good, and their store is only about 10 miles from my house. They have a great selection of discs including low cost misprints.

Marshal Street Another good choice for price and selection. You can also pick color and weight, and they have the **best flight guide** for choosing discs.

Clearwater disc golf. Another good choice. Prices are

good and shipping was quick when I have ordered from them.

Sun King. Prices are good. I have bought from them 1 time, no problems

Par 72 disc golf. Run by Timmy Gill who is a pro disc golfer and course designer in the upper Midwest. Good prices.

Prime Discs. You can pick exact weight and color. Prices good, good website.

These are the places I have used to buy discs. This doesn't mean there aren't many other great places to buy, these are the biggest. I have ordered from them and been happy with the service I received.

How to talk disc golf

The more I practice, the luckier I get. Jerry Barber

Disc Golf Lingo

Most people who play disc golf know the regular terms and language. There are lots of other words that people use for describing things that happen on the course, that are not in the dictionary, or in the general vocabulary for disc golf. I have gathered some interesting terms from other players, and from what I've read that other players use. I will share the common ones, along with some of the better ones that are not common.

Common disc golf language

Ace Getting the disc in the basket on the first shot.

Hyzer Releasing the disc with the edge closest to your body, higher than the other edge.

Anhyzer The outside edge is higher than the inside edge.

Over stable The disc wants to hyzer into the ground when you release it. To make it not hyzer you must snap it and throw it hard, with a slight anhyzer.

Under stable Can throw with less spin, less snap to fly

strait, will not go as far and is not as good in the wind.

Turnover When you throw the disc hard with good snap, it will turn opposite the way it is meant to turn. If you're throwing RHBH it will turn to the right.

S Curve The flight of the disc starts as an anhyzer, and then will hyzer at the end of the flight.

Snap The amount of spin on the disc at release from your hand.

Driving, The throw from the tee box.

Approach The shot from the drive to the basket.

Putt Throwing the disc into the basket.

Grip How you hold the disc when you're throwing.

Player Invented disc golf Terms

Dead Man - when your putt hits the side of the basket and drops to the ground.

Chain Smoking - Several great putts in a row.

Bogey Sandwich - A scorecard with a par bogey, bogey

par.

Black Ace- Acing the wrong hole.

Cabbage - The weeds in the rough.

Chastity belt - the yellow band on the Innova baskets.

Clank - The sound that a putt makes when it hits the chastity belt.

Doink – A putt that hits the number plate.

Hit the nickel - when your putt hits the number plate.

Horking -A huge long throw.

Locals route: taking an unconventional path gets you to the basket.

Lumberjacking - when you're hitting every tree.

Mirkwood Very thick woods.

Nickel – A score of 5 on a hole.

Nuclear shule –Very thick rough.

Fly-By: putt correct height, but sails by the basket.

Fluke deuce- A 2 from something very lucky happening.

Gaack miss a short putt.

Grenade- A shot that is high and falls fast to the ground.

Head Banger - when your drive lands under the basket and you might bang your head on the basket as you pick it up.

More disc golf terms

Paper plate An understable disc.

Pig-Putt . A putt that's really bad.

Pinball – a shot that hits more than 1 tree.

Pinball Wizard – continually hitting multiple trees.

Rooted - when the tree root stops your shot from skipping.

Saturn - a score of 6 (6th planet)

Shank- any shot that does not do what you wanted.

Shule - heavy weeds off the fairway

Sneak- in flight instruction to the disc.

Snob – a throw with the nose of the disc up.

Snowman - A score of 8.

Spinach – bushes, trees, and undergrowth.

Taco - To hit a tree so hard it folds like a taco.

Tombstone- a disc golf disc that hits the ground, and remains standing on edge,

Tournament Roll - When your disc hits the basket and rolls farther away.

Tree flection - the tree gives you a good deflection.

Valet service - When you park your drive under the basket.

CFR - Candy Fundraiser.

CTP - Closest drive to the Pole

DL- Dead Last in the order.

FAT - When you hit the First Available Tree

LB - Lucky Bounce.

SED - Seeing Eye Disc.

YSA - You're Still Away

Gust from the Gods - when the wind blows the disc way off line.

Gettin' Greasy...... sneakin through the trees.

Lawn Dart - a disc that has landed partially buried in the ground.

Merked when you get hit in the head from someone's throw off of the tee

Tombstone for those discs that stick edge-on into muddy/soft ground.

Helicopter - A shot that needs to come straight down at the end without curving.

A rip - The perfect drive.

Best training videos

Picking your first discs

Understanding off axis torque

How to do the X step

Before and after the game with Liz Carr

5 Tips to save 5 Strokes

Putt like Paul McBeth

Dave Feldberg putting clinic

Getting out of trouble

Overhead shots

Tips on grips with Dave Feldberg

Approach shots

Backhand distance tips

Long distance driving

Distance driving techniques

Distance driving with Dion Arlyn

Monster distance with Avery Jenkins

Forehand driving techniques

Forehand drives with Mark Ellis

Sidearm drives with Avery Jenkins

Putting with Todd Erickson

Making long putts with Mark Ellis

Putting tips with Dave Dunipace

Driving with Dan Beato

Backhand drives with Avery Jenkins

Throwing basics

Driving clinic with Jay Reading

Throwing a hyzer flip

Grip Tips

Throwing a roller

Beginner grip basics

Throwing tomahawks

Dave Feldbergs towel tip for getting snap

The mental game with Avery Jenkins

There are other disc golf tip videos on YouTube, but if you master the techniques that are showed in these videos, you will be a great disc golfer. Enjoy.

Thank you for reading my book. This is a book you should hang onto and keep where you can use it as a reference book when you need to work on a part of your game.

If you enjoyed the book and think it can help disc golfers improve their game, please go to **Amazon and write a review** about the book so others will read it.

Thanks

Made in the USA
Columbia, SC
13 January 2018